OREGON TRAIL

Volume 1

Tales of the Wild West Series

Rick Steber

Illustrations by Don Gray

NOTE
OREGON TRAIL is the first book in the
Tales of the Wild West Series

OREGON TRAIL
Volume 1
Tales of the Wild West Series

Bonanza Publishing
Box 204
Prineville, Oregon 97754

Tales of the Wild West

INTRODUCTION

Historians recognize 1843 as the official beginning of the Oregon Trail. That spring a thousand pioneers, traveling in 120 wagons, departed from Elm Grove, Missouri. When the pioneers reached the Columbia River they built rafts and flat-bottomed boats to float their wagons through the dangerous rapids of the Columbia Gorge to the Willamette Valley.

The heyday of the trail occurred after gold was discovered in California in 1848. It is estimated that more than 300,000 people traveled the Oregon Trail by covered wagon and that as many as one in ten died along the way from illness, accidents and other misfortunes.

The Oregon Trail was a big, wide trail that followed the general lay of the land with a series of landmarks serving as beacons to guide the travelers. Wagon emigrants used this route until the era ended with the advent of mass-produced automobiles in the early 1900s.

Today stretches of the Oregon Trail remain visible as ruts; ruts carved into the earth, worn by time and masked by wildflowers, sagebrush and trees.

THE PRAIRIE SCHOONER

Some ordered their prairie schooners brand new from the factory; others simply had the local blacksmith make the necessary adjustments on the farm wagon.

The Conestoga wagon, which originated in Pennsylvania in the mid-1700s, was a popular prairie schooner. It was big and roomy but it was also heavy and for that reason many emigrant guidebooks recommended the Yankee wagon for traveling the Oregon Trail. The Yankee was made of well-seasoned, close-grained oak and could be purchased for about $200.

Families heading west spent many days readying their wagons, filling them with everything they could possibly need for a five-month journey. When packing was completed, a canvas cover was stretched over the top. If the pioneers followed the advice of experienced guides, the coverings were always doubled to provide greater protection against the weather.

A wagon was worthless unless it had good wheels and Joel Palmer, who led many wagon trains westward, suggested, "Wagon wheels should be at least one and three-quarters inches wide; three inches would be best of all for crossing the oftentimes loose, sandy roads. The rims should be, at the minimum, three-quarters of an inch thick and fastened to the felloes with bolts rather than nails. Hub boxes should be at least four inches thick."

If the prairie schooner were well-seasoned and well-made and the oxen faithful and strong, the pioneers had a fighting chance to reach their destinations with a wagon that could be used for chores and transportation on their new farms in the West.

WAGONS WEST

The spring of 1845 three thousand people were gathered near St. Joseph, Missouri, anxious to begin their overland journey into the unknown. Joel Palmer, leader of one of the wagon trains, informed the pioneers: "The loading should consist of provisions and apparel, a necessary supply of cooking fixtures, a few tools ... everything in the outfit should be as light as the required strength will permit, no useless trumpery should be taken."

The pioneers had to plan for more than a five-month, 2,000-mile cross-country journey. Everything that was necessary to build a new home and to begin farming also had to be packed. Palmer suggested the minimum food essentials for each adult consist of two hundred pounds of flour, seventy-five pounds of bacon, ten pounds of rice, five pounds of coffee, twenty-five pounds of sugar, ten pounds of salt, two bushels of dried beans and dried fruit, one bushel of corn and corn meal and one keg of vinegar.

Good shoes and warm clothes were a requirement and each man was required to carry a rifle and plenty of ammunition. Oxen were considered the best animals to pull the heavy wagons; they were strong and dependable and Indians were not likely to steal them.

By the middle of April, with men driving the stubborn green teams, women and babies crowding into the wagons, the older children walking and driving the loose stock, the long caravan of wagons started west.

3

OXEN AND BUFFALO

While crossing the broad sweep of the plains the early pioneers discovered a curious fact about oxen. Oxen go absolutely crazy when smelling buffalo.

One pioneer related, "It is an odd thing that when oxen smell the fresh trail of the buffalo they paw and bellow as if they smelt fresh blood. If you have ever tried to stop a runaway oxen team, you know what hard work it is."

An 1845 wagon train, captained by Presley Welch, had the misfortune of a runaway. At first the driver tried to thwart the headlong charge by pulling on the heavy yoke and poking at the oxen with a stick. Outriders came alongside and tried to turn the lumbering animals but they plowed ahead over the uneven ground.

The wagon bounced along behind in sharp jolts like the popping of a whip. In this mad dash two oxen ran themselves to death. When the runaway was finally stopped the dead animals were butchered. The pioneers found the meat "tough and stringy".

Later in the journey the guide came riding at a dead gallop, shouting to swing the wagons into a circle and corral the oxen inside. He said a herd of buffalo was stampeding and would be there within minutes.

The herd passed dangerously close to the circle of wagons and the oxen were frantic, trying repeatedly to join the stampeding buffalo, but none were able. The pioneers were forced to stay in camp several hours until the guides deemed the oxen would be manageable.

WAGON TRAIN JUSTICE

John Smith was a disagreeable old cuss and as the wagons of the Missouri company pulled out of St. Joe that spring morning in 1852, he cursed the others because they raised dust.

Along the way to Oregon a young boy was orphaned. Old man Smith took the boy in. From the very beginning he belittled the boy, complaining — among other things — that the lad was depleting his stock of rations. It seemed that the boy could do nothing right. The oxen received too little or too much feed. The cook fire was either too hot or not hot enough.

For his part the boy tried. Others in the wagon train often came to his defense. They advised Smith to change his ways. Smith rebuffed them, saying he would do whatever he pleased.

As the journey progressed it seemed as though the division between the man and the boy became more and more pronounced. One day the boy was walking alongside the wagon. A wheel fell off and Smith flew into a rage, accusing the boy of causing it. At night camp Smith was overheard muttering, "I'll fix him."

In the morning Smith seemed to have reversed his mood and cheerily asked the boy if he would like to go rabbit hunting. The man and the boy walked away from the wagon train. The boy never returned.

The old man stood trial for murder and was found guilty. Since there were no trees, three wagons were pushed together and the tongues lifted to form a triangle. A rope was fastened to the top of the tongues, a noose fashioned and wagon train justice ran its swift course.

5

A HARD TRAIL

William Smith, his wife and their nine children, were Oregon Trail pioneers of 1846. They were with a group attempting to blaze a new trail to Oregon over the Applegate Cutoff.

They reached the Umpqua River drainage when a freak windstorm struck and downed trees blocked further passage by the wagons. It was suggested the wagons be abandoned and that the oxen could be ridden to safety.

William Smith told the others, "I've got a wife and nine children. My daughter Louisa is deathly sick and you know my son Thaddeus is crippled and cannot ride. I am taking my wagon. I know we can make it. But maybe I'm the only man among us with any guts."

As William was exhorting the others he suddenly sank to his knees, grabbed at his chest, cried, "Lord, have mercy upon me!" and died.

The wagon that William had been so determined to take to the end of the trail was torn apart and used to make his coffin. His wife cried over his grave and then packed her nine children on the two oxen and continued the journey.

Along the way little Louisa's condition deteriorated. The last words Louisa whispered to her mother were, "Bury me deep, pile rocks on top. I don't want the wolves to get me."

Somehow Ellen was able to make it safely to the Willamette Valley with the remainder of her family intact. Starting with a donation land claim she carved out an existence and raised her eight children.

THE NAME

Solomon Trumble started west over the Oregon Trail with the intention of claiming a homestead in Oregon and then sending for his family. A year passed and his family did not receive any letters from him.

During that year his daughter married George Masiker and shortly after the wedding George informed his bride they would soon be moving to Oregon. They joined a wagon train and for several weeks they traveled along the Platte River.

After supper one evening Mrs. Masiker completed her chores and decided to go for a walk. George warned her, "Don't go wandering far. Stay within sight of the wagons."

She walked a short distance, sat on a large flat rock near the river and watched the Sandhill cranes fly over. She listened to their strange, shrill voices and as the sun began to set in a fiery glow of yellows and reds she tried to imagine what Oregon must look like. She remembered her father and the things he had said; that it was always green and the soil was black as coal and the weather conducive to farming. The daydream ended as the sun tumbled from the sky.

Mrs. Masiker started back for camp but on the way she noticed the shoulder blade of a buffalo stuck in the ground, marking a grave. She could see writing on the bleached bone and bent to read the faded lead markings. There was a name — Solomon Trumble — her father.

THE PINE BOX

Grandma Gaylord was crying as she bent and gave Leonora a kiss goodbye. The wagon started forward and the little girl hurried to catch up with her folks and the other members of the Illinois wagon train. They were off to Oregon.

That afternoon they came to a long hill and the women and children stepped down from the wagons to save the oxen from having to pull their weight. Leonora, taking a nap in the wagon, awoke with a start to find her mother and her sisters no longer there.

Leonora pulled back a corner of the canvas cover and saw the others walking off to the side of the wagon away from the billowing dust. She swung her legs over the sideboard and was going to drop to the ground but the wagon hit a chuckhole and Leonora lost her balance and fell. The rear wheel passed over her leg and the small thighbone snapped under the heavy weight of the wagon. She cried out in pain.

There was a doctor on the wagon train and he set Leonora's broken leg and ordered that a narrow pine box be built, giving precise measurements so the injured leg would fit in it very tightly.

Leonora traveled with her leg in the pine box all the way to Oregon. Sixty-four years later, in 1917, she was honored by the Oregon Pioneer Association. They noted that Leonora had come west in a pine box and lived to tell about it.

MERCY ARROW

On the way west a Missourian left the wagon train he had been traveling with to spend a few days trapping in the high country. He was warned he was entering Blackfoot territory and he promised to be careful.

The wagons continued west while the lone Missourian drifted north into the snowy mountains, setting beaver traps in likely spots. After several successful days, and after having come across neither Indians nor Indian sign, the man felt safe.

One afternoon he was knee deep in water retrieving a drowned beaver. His rifle was out of reach on the bank. Suddenly he felt a strange sensation, as though he were being watched. He looked up and saw that a party of mounted Indians, their faces dabbed with paint, had him surrounded.

The Missourian was marched to the Indian camp and held under guard. That night the Indians danced and held council. The Missourian, concerned about his fate, asked the Indian guard what was happening. He was told, "Talk about you die."

The Missourian was resigned to the fact he would be killed but he wanted to know how. The guard answered, "You burn."

The white man pleaded with the guard. "I'm not afraid to die but I don't want to burn to death. Kill me now." The guard said nothing.

A great quantity of firewood was heaped around a lone tree. The Missourian was led forward. He was tied to the tree. Again he pleaded, "Shoot me."

Coals were brought from the fire and the pyre was ignited. Flames were licking at the Missourian's feet when an arrow whistled through the air and stuck him in the heart. The fire consumed a dead man.

BAD APPLE

A wagon train was headed west with one man in the group who constantly grumbled, complained and found fault with everything. He was a bad apple.

One of this man's pet peeves was the welcoming manner in which members of the wagon train greeted the Indians they met along the way. He was fond of saying, "The only way to treat an Indian is to shoot first and ask if he is friendly later on."

The wagon train passed an Indian village on the upper reaches of the Platte River. The emigrants enlisted the services of an Indian to guide them. The bad apple picked a fight with the guide and that night a single rifle shot resounded. The body of the Indian was discovered at the edge of camp and the bad apple could not be found.

Some members of the wagon train wanted to bury the Indian and go on their way. Others felt if they buried the Indian his tribe would come looking, discover the grave and assume the worst. It was decided one among them would return the body to the Indian village and explain the circumstances. To be fair, straws were drawn.

The next morning the wagon train continued west while the unlucky man rode east with the body of the dead Indian lashed to the back of his saddle. When he reached the Indian village he was immediately escorted to the chief's tepee. The chief listened to the explanation, accepted the body and made signs the white man was free to leave. He did so. But he was followed by a delegation of Indians who stayed with him until they reached the point where the Indian had been killed.

Here they broke away from the Oregon Trail and began searching. Before long a shot was fired. The Indians had found the bad apple.

DEATH ON THE TRAIL

During the year 1852 fatal cholera wiped out ten percent of the emigrants as they made their way west over the Oregon Trail. Seven persons in one family were buried in a single grave. A scout reported that following from the Platte River to Fort Laramie, a distance of 400 miles, he had counted nearly 5,000 graves.

Death rode with the Abbott family in 1852. Their wagon made it as far as the Platte River before the father became sick and soon died of dreaded cholera. He left behind a wife and five children.

"We laid him to rest where the Old Emigrant road left the fork of Little Blue River and passed on," wrote John Abbott, one of the sons.

"The cholera claimed able-bodied men, women and children by the score. Panic prevailed. You could see men and women on their bended knees asking God to show mercy on their loved ones.

"Our family's only fatality passing through the cholera belt was Father. But as a whole the train lost 30 percent.

"We reached the Snake River, which was a region where mountain fever was prevalent, and Mother took ill. She died and we buried her on the banks of the Powder River. From then on us five kids were on our own. When things like that happen it makes you grow up in a hurry.

"We made it, reached the Willamette Valley, and ever after this has been home — the promised land."

LONG TIME IN COMING

Even before they reached the starting point of the Oregon Trail the William McCown family suffered misfortune. The Mississippi river steamer on which they took passage hit a floating snag and began to take on water. The captain turned toward shore and in the excitement he steered for Illinois though the wagon emigrants wanted to land on the Missouri side. An old riverboat captain, on board as a passenger, wrestled the wheel away and steered for Missouri. The steamer ran aground and, although the passengers escaped unharmed, the steamer sank and all possessions were lost.

The young McCown family was destitute but William was able to find a job in a blacksmith shop. He worked there until he had earned enough money to purchase a two-wheel cart. Supplies were loaded in the cart and the family started west again, stopping several times while William found employment. They were in Henry County, then Post Oak and on to Kansas. William's wife died there.

By the time they reached the Cascades snow was on the pass on the Barlow toll road, but William elected to try to make the crossing. For several days they were trapped in a blizzard but when the weather cleared they fought their way over the top and down into the Willamette Valley.

The McCowns spent that winter camped in the hills near Oregon City. Only one animal, the saddle horse, survived and when spring finally arrived he became a plow horse.

SLAVE WOMAN

As Oregon-bound emigrants were being organized near St. Joseph, Missouri a few families and friends decided they could make better time on their own without the inconvenience of being part of a large wagon train. They moved a few miles ahead of the main body.

Three days after jumping off from St. Joseph the group made camp, ate supper and went to bed without taking the precaution of setting a night guard.

Around midnight Indians sneaked into camp, surprised the sleeping pioneers and set fire to their wagons. Only two members of the party were spared, a woman and her twelve-year-old son.

The woman was set on an Indian pony and her son was placed behind her. As the pony was led from the terrifying scene the woman looked back and saw her husband move his hand. She whispered to her son, told him his father was still alive and that when she tapped him on the leg he was to drop off the side of the pony and hide in the grass. When it was safe he was to run back to the main wagon train for help.

The Indians, excited at the successful raid, did not notice the boy escape. He ran with fear pushing him and along the way he overtook his father, who was crawling on hands and knees.

The woman remained captive for a number of years. She suffered and endured a great deal, but because of the unceasing efforts of her husband and son she eventually was rescued by a group of trappers who purchased her from the Indians.

BRAVERY

Miralda Greenstreet was alone, two miles behind the Oregon-bound wagon train, driving the loose stock. They were in Indian country and Miralda, mindful of the danger, kept checking around her for signs of trouble.

Without warning a war party of fifty Indians boiled over a nearby ridge. They wore paint on their faces and brandished rifles and bows and arrows. Miralda knew it would be fruitless to try to outrun the Indians so she elected to slip from her saddle and stand, clutching her horse's reins.

The Indians rode up to her. They peered at this brave young woman and Miralda met their gaze, masking her terror behind a calm exterior. Her reins were jerked away. The Indians spun their ponies in unison and raced toward a spot a hundred yards away. They arranged themselves in pairs and with a string of sharp yips and blood-curdling whoops they came straight at Miralda. As they passed on either side they swung tomahawks at her head. They flashed so close it whistled the air and made her skin crawl.

Pass after pass the war party continued this chilling game, waiting for Miralda's own fear to cause her to flinch. But she stood as still as a stone statue.

At last the braves tired of their macabre fun. They came in and made a tight circle around her. One of them spoke. He said, "Brave squaw." Then they rode away, leaving Miralda absolutely alone on the broad sweep of the plains.

PEGLEG

During the Civil War a fellow by the name of Simpson lost a leg and had it replaced with a wooden peg. Most everyone took to calling him Pegleg.

Pegleg came over the Oregon Trail in 1866. He was the brunt of most of the jokes because in addition to his obvious handicap, he also stuttered and was painfully shy. When word got around that Pegleg had an unnatural fear of Indians, it only made matters worse. There were a few demented souls who took delight in sneaking up behind Pegleg and giving a war whoop just to laugh at his nervous reaction.

One afternoon, while crossing a marshy area within sight of Fort Laramie, Pegleg's wagon became mired in mud. The other wagons were a mile away when someone took notice and a small group went back to help him free the wagon.

The men were halfway there when Indians suddenly appeared and began circling Pegleg's wagon. Shots were fired and there was Pegleg, standing in the bed of his wagon with the canvas cover tossed back, turning this way and that, bravely standing his ground while shooting at the Indians. The Indians hastily departed.

Luckily for Pegleg he was able to free himself before the men from the wagon train reached him. He never confessed that his wooden leg had been caught in a knothole in the bed of the wagon and he had been forced to make the best of a bad situation. Instead, he basked in their warm accolades commending his courage.

DOWN TO LONG JOHNS

Andrew Masters was a troubled man. His wife was expecting their firstborn any day and if they stayed with the wagon train it would take at least a week before they reached Doctor Whitman's mission.

Andrew knew they could travel much faster by saddle horse and the following morning, as they were breaking camp in the Grande Ronde Valley, he and his wife departed on horseback. The wagon emigrants waved and called encouragement.

For two days they traveled through the Blue Mountains. On the morning of the third day they awoke to find their horses missing. Mrs. Masters said she did not want to give birth if the baby was doomed. Soon, two Indians rode into camp. They claimed to know where the horses were and offered to trade.

"We don't have anything to trade," Andrew informed them. One of the Indians suggested a deal could be struck if Andrew were willing to part with his shirt, trousers and the red bandana he wore around his neck.

Within an hour the Indians returned with the horses and Andrew disrobed down to his longjohns. He and his wife rode on. They reached the mission and Mrs. Masters immediately went under Doctor Whitman's care. The following morning she gave birth to a strong, healthy baby.

FIREWORKS

Monroe Stayles, his wife and their daughter Inez, came west over the Oregon Trail. They crossed the Cascades on the Barlow toll road and arrived at Oregon City thinking the excitement of the journey was over.

A level spot near the Willamette River was chosen as a camping spot and the Stayles family went about evening chores. It did not bother Monroe when a few Indians, who were camped nearby, paid a visit. He figured Indians living so close to civilization must be friendly. But then he saw how much attention one of the Indians, the chief, was paying to Inez.

Inez was only twelve years old but her appearance belied her age. She had raven-black hair, dark eyes and was very pretty. The chief fell in love with her.

Indian tradition dictated a man trade for his bride. The chief approached Monroe, told him of his intentions and offered robes, horses and furs in exchange for the girl. Monroe ran him out of camp.

It was nearly dark when Mrs. Stayles went to the nearby spring for a pail of water. She did not return and Monroe was about to look for her when an Indian came into camp with the message that Mrs. Stayles was being held captive and would be released only after Inez was given to the chief.

Thinking quickly, Monroe told the messenger, "Tell your chief if my wife is not returned immediately the Great Spirit will make fire come down like rain on your village."

The Indian departed. Monroe retrieved a small box of fireworks that he had brought all the way from home. He walked toward the Indian village and when he was still a hundred yards out, he lit the first rocket. It went high into the night sky and exploded. Before another rocket could be launched Mrs. Stayles was set free.

BOILED BUFFALO HIDE

A small group of friends came west together. They endured the long wagon trip and at The Dalles took a raft for the remainder of the journey down the Columbia River.

Coming through Cascades Rapids a strong wind hit their raft from the side and capsized them. They were thrown in the icy water and forced to swim for their lives.

By some miracle all landed safely on a narrow strip of shoreline that butted up against a rock wall several hundred feet high. They quickly got down to the basics of survival. One man had flint and was able to start a fire with driftwood. A boiling pot and a buffalo hide happened to wash ashore and since the hide was the only thing remotely associated with food they scraped off the hair, cut the hide into strips, and placed the strips in the pot to boil.

At Fort Vancouver, friends were awaiting their arrival. When the raft did not reach its destination they became worried and arranged for Indians to search the river. They located the lost group on their solitary spit of beach and rescued them. The little group had spent seven days and nights on the isolated beach, subsisting only on the boiled buffalo hide.

MASSACRE ROCKS

Twenty-five Iowa families made up the small wagon train that reached Fort Hall the first of August 1862. That night the fiddle was brought out and the pioneers danced and celebrated having come 1,200 miles. But they knew that the most difficult part of the journey lay ahead: crossing the Snake River plains and over the Blue Mountains and the Cascade Mountains to reach the promised land in the Willamette Valley.

The wagon train followed along on the south side of the Snake River for several days. Late one afternoon the lead driver spotted Palisade. Word was relayed from one wagon to the next that the prominent landmark was close at hand.

Palisade, an unusual rock formation, obstructed the course of the Oregon Trail. The wagons were forced to line out in single file as they detoured on a winding course through the rocks.

Upon reaching the narrowest spot rifle shots rang out and a volley of arrows was launched in the direction of the wagon train. A war party of Indians was hiding among the rocks and they fired at the emigrants again and again. The pioneers could not circle their wagons. They could not even turn around. They whipped the oxen and tried to charge through the narrow passageway.

Nine emigrants were killed in the ambush. Ever after, Palisade has been known as Massacre Rocks.

THE PRICE WAS DEATH

The Winters family was coming west and having a tough time of it. Dreaded cholera struck their wagon train. Hiram Winters watched for symptoms in his wife Rebecca and the children but sickness passed them by until one evening near Scotts Bluff, Nebraska. As they made camp Rebecca complained that she was not feeling well. She said her stomach hurt and a short time later she claimed she was dizzy. She laid down on the bed in the wagon while Hiram cooked dinner.

The swiftness of the disease took the family by surprise. One minute Rebecca was resting comfortably and the next she was having difficulty breathing. Just before midnight Hiram took a cup of broth to her and discovered she had died.

Hiram mourned the loss by keeping his hands busy. He took a spare wagon rim, picked up a hammer and metal chisel and in the firelight he began etching a grave marker for Rebecca.

Hiram finished his work as the sun came over the horizon. Etched on the rounded rim were the words, "Rebecca Winters, age 50 years". Rebecca was buried and the rim was used to mark the grave. For many years the rim endured as a shrine to the memory of a wife and mother who gave her life crossing the Oregon Trail.

THE CANNON AND
THE MULE MOLLY

Not a day passed that members of the small wagon train did not fear Indian attack. But across the Plains and even over the Rocky Mountains the Indians they encountered were friendly. And then they hit the Oregon Country.

On a sagebrush flat, cut by deep dry washes that could hide men on horseback, came a blood-curdling whoop and the pounding noise of horses on the move. A large party of Indians emerged from a dry wash. Their faces were painted and they were well armed. They fired arrows as they galloped the length of the wagon train.

The captain called for the wagons to be circled and drivers quickly obeyed. But even after the wagons had been pulled into a protective circle the attack persisted. The Indians rode in close, shooting arrows while the pioneers returned fire with black powder rifles.

The pioneers had planned for a moment like this. Before leaving Missouri they had purchased a small cannon and a mule named Molly to carry it. Molly was led to an opening between wagons and without taking time to unpack her, the cannon was loaded and Molly turned so that her hindquarters, as well as the opening of the cannon, were pointed toward the Indians.

White smoke belched from the cannon when it was fired and Molly kicked up her heels. Almost immediately the Indian chief held up his right arm, signaling for a truce. He slowly rode forward.

Upon reaching the wagon train he spoke solemnly, saying the pioneers were free to go, that the Indians could not hope to compete against the white man who could "shootum mule".

TRAIL OF FEATHERS

In 1854 members of a wagon train to Oregon had several encounters with hostile Indians. One of those occurred when they came across several cabins scattered around a spring.

They stopped and called but could not raise anyone. That seemed strange and upon investigation it was discovered that the cabins had been ransacked and the inhabitants were missing.

"Let's look around," suggested one of the men. They fanned out in the sagebrush looking for tracks or other sign but found nothing until one of the searchers discovered a feather. This led to another feather, and another, and another. Evidently a leaky feather mattress had been part of the plunder.

Several men were left to guard the wagons and to protect the women and children while the others rode along the trail of feathers. They proceeded slowly through foothills until at last they came to a high ridge. They dismounted and crawled to a position where they could peer over the edge without being skylined. In the valley below they saw Indians dancing around a fire, and lying face down in the dirt, hands bound behind their backs, were a number of white men.

The pioneers pulled back and an attack plan was quickly scratched on the ground. They would surround the Indian camp and swoop in from all directions at once. The plan worked perfectly and the settlers, to the last man, were rescued.

BUFFALO WALL

Buffalo stampedes struck fear into the hearts of the early-day pioneers. A fellow by the name of Crabtree gave a personal account of living through a buffalo stampede.

He told how a line of dust, stretching from horizon to horizon, was the first detectable sign of a buffalo stampede. How, from so many hooves striking the earth, there came the sound of distant rolling thunder. There was no hope of avoiding the stampede, all they could do was circle the wagons and take actions to try to split the herd.

Crabtree claimed, "I had the fastest horse in camp. He was high strung and fast. I led the charge. We fired our guns in the air, but to no avail. And when the herd threatened to over-run me I turned around and ran with it. To me it seemed like trying to outrun a flood.

"My horse went down. He probably hit a gopher hole. I got knocked off, was dazed there for a second, looked up and saw the buffalo were almost on me. I managed to crawl over against my horse. A couple of buffalo went around me, one tried to leap over the top and hung up. After that it was like dominoes as bodies piled up, around and over me. I didn't move.

"The herd swept past, the thunder was going away and the choking dust was beginning to settle when I was able to squirm my way from beneath the mass of dead and dying buffalo. I fully expected the wagons to have been obliterated by the stampede. But to my complete and utter amazement it was safe, spared because my buffalo wall had split the herd on either side of the circle of wagons."

SAVED BY A DOUGHNUT

Upon crossing the Snake River the 36 members of the Ohio train felt like celebrating. Wagons were circled and the women began cooking a special dinner while the men stood around in groups discussing the potential of the Willamette Valley.

A small girl was the first to see the Indians and call out a warning. The Indians greatly outnumbered the pioneers. They sat motionless on their ponies. Finally the chief, who was wearing a headdress made from eagle feathers, rode to the edge of the circle of wagons. A woman stepped forward with a plate of hot doughnuts. She held it toward the chief.

He eyed it distrustfully. Thinking quickly the woman began distributing doughnuts among members of her party. They ate with exaggerated relish, rubbing their stomachs and smacking their lips to make their pleasure most apparent.

Again the woman approached the chief but still he refused. She offered doughnuts to the warriors. One young brave had the nerve to grab one and take a taste. He must have enjoyed it because he ate it in two tremendous bites. The Indians dismounted and the remaining doughnuts were quickly consumed.

The women fried a vast quantity of doughnuts and while the feast was in progress all thought of war between the parties was forgotten. When it was over the Indians rode away and in the morning the Ohio wagon train continued on to the Willamette Valley.

THE WORST MEMORY

Eva Brown wrote how her father traveled west from Wisconsin in the 1800s and that her mother, brother and she joined him later, after he had found a place to live.

"We traveled by train to the end of the road, which was Rosebud, Montana," she said. "From there we went by wagon. There were many times on the way to Oregon I had to walk. I thought I had a reasonably heavy pair of shoes but they did not hold up. Crossing the desert, cactus stuck me through the soles of those shoes and in the mountains I had to walk barefoot through the snow.

"When we got to where we were going we found Father had built a frame house, although lumber was hard to come by. Our beds were boards nailed together and mattresses were straw ticks. We brought currant shrubs and potatoes with us from Wisconsin. Father planted them and they did very well.

"Father and Mother filed on a preemption claim and so did my brother and I. All the family lived there together, where the claims joined in the middle of the wilderness.

"I remember the rattlesnakes. Oh, Lordy, do I remember the rattlesnakes! The worst moment of my life was the time in the dark when I reached down to take the eggs from under a hen and found a rattler all coiled up there in the nest. Oh my, that frightened me terribly."

WOMEN OF THE TRAIL

The women of the Oregon Trail are often perceived in one of two ways: as a hardy, rawboned woman who walked beside the wagon cradling a nursing baby in one arm and firing a rifle at savage Indians with the other; or a pale Eastern-bred woman who had fallen in love with a wandering man and would follow him anywhere.

But the women who came West were more than stereotypes. They cried over the loss of loved ones and sometimes moaned under the hardships of the trail. One woman, who gave birth along the way, looked back on the crossing as an "adventure". Another wrote it was "the high point of my life".

When they arrived in Oregon the women were just as busy as on the trail. While men cleared fields and planted crops the women cooked, washed, and made homes in the wilderness.

One woman wrote in her diary, "My husband would have turned back a hundred times on the trail and a hundred times since we landed but I won't let him."

Another myth is that pioneer women were in constant danger from Indians. The fact was that women often traded with the Indians, exchanging fresh homemade bread for wild meat, milk and doughnuts for salmon. Only during times of war were Indians a threat.

One pioneer woman looked back on the early years and claimed, "Never was there a day I wished myself back East to live."

GAMES

The children of the Oregon Trail had to leave most of their toys behind, but there was no lack of imagination when it came to finding new playthings along the way.

One of the favorite games of young boys on a wagon train in 1843 was played with the swollen paunch of a slaughtered ox.

Jesse Applegate, who was seven years old, described how the game was played. "The sport consisted in running and butting your head against the paunch and being bounced back, the recoil being in proportion to the force of contact."

It became a favorite game as youngsters showed their courage by running and jumping harder and harder. There was not a particular name for the game until the day a boy named Andy, with cries of, "Give her goss, Andy," ringing in his ears, jumped at the paunch harder than anyone had dared.

Jesse Applegate told what happened. "Andy backed off much farther than anyone had before, and then charged the paunch at the top of his speed, and when within a couple of yards of the target, leaped up from the ground and came down like a pile driver against the paunch, but he did not bounce back. The stomach had closed so tightly around his neck that he could not withdraw his head. We took hold of his legs and pulled him out, but the joke was on Andy and 'Give her goss, Andy' was a favorite game among the boys long after."

FINDING A HORSE

William Savage was a young man walking to Oregon in the company of a wagon train. Every step he took made him wish he had a horse.

Near the crossing of the Sweetwater River he spotted a mount, saddled and tied to a tree some distance off the trail. William called to Captain Umphlette and said he was going to retrieve the horse.

"It's an Indian trick. I've seen 'em use it before to lure a man away from the train. I can't let you go, William," the captain stated.

"I respect your decision," William told him. But after thinking for a moment he suggested, "We should not leave the trap baited and have someone from a following train killed. I better shoot the horse."

He took a prone position for the long shot, but instead of killing the horse the bullet kicked up dirt under its belly. The frightened horse pulled loose and began running in a big circle that brought him near the wagon train. William jumped to his feet, ran forward, grabbed the lead rope and took control of the horse.

The wagon train continued, and riding in the front of the column was William Savage. He was the envy of the others as he rode the horse all the way to Oregon.

William settled in the Willamette Valley, became a stockman and later a banker in Dallas. The horse that carried him to Oregon was turned out to pasture and eventually died of old age.

STARTING OUT

Bill Patton was a young Missourian who fell in love with a girl named Annie Dickens. When Annie's parents decided to emigrate to Oregon, young Bill lost no time signing on as an oxen driver on the same wagon train.

Bill courted Annie and one night, with the stars out and the coyotes howling, he asked her to marry him when they reached Oregon.

Somewhere along the way, the money Bill had managed to save was stolen. He couldn't get married until he was financially secure so when they reached the Willamette Valley he went to work splitting rails for 37¢ per hundred. After he had earned $2.25 he made the necessary arrangements to marry Annie.

The day after the ceremony Bill went back to splitting rails. One day his father-in-law talked to him about the merits of owning land. He also said he would like to have his daughter close by and told Bill the land adjacent to his donation land claim was open for claiming.

When Bill went to file on the land he discovered a fellow by the name of Center had just filed on it. Bill looked up Center. Center listened to the boy, thought about it for a moment and concluded land was available everywhere. Each acre was just as good as the next as far as he was concerned. "All right, lad. I'll sell," he told Bill. "The price for my 160 acres will be one plug of tobacco."

The deal was struck. In the following years Bill and Annie raised nine Patton children on the home place.

SIGN OF DISTRESS

"In the early spring of 1852, we started for Oregon," related pioneer J.C. Moreland. "There were about 40 wagons in our train. Our company held together until we reached the Grande Ronde Valley, and those who could travel faster left us behind to shift for ourselves. I remember very distinctly climbing in the mountains and our oxen were so weak we had to throw out everything we could possibly do without.

"One scene stands out particularly strongly in my mind. We had eaten the last of our hardtack and the last of our bacon. We were without provisions of any kind. I was sitting on a log near the wagon, hunger gnawing at my stomach. Rain was falling. I was cold and discouraged.

"I heard a noise and with a boy's curiosity I went down the trail to investigate. I came running back and excitedly told the folks, 'Here comes a man on a fat horse and a fat yoke of oxen pulling his wagon.'

"When he drove up, Father spoke to him and made a sign with his hands I did not understand. The man promptly took several loaves of light bread as well as some boiled beef, cold boiled potatoes and raw onions from his wagon and gave them to Mother. I never ate a better meal in my entire life.

"Afterward I asked my father what made the man give us the food since I knew we had no money to pay for it. Father said, 'My boy, I gave him the Master Mason sign of distress.'

"Right then and there I decided to become a Mason."

FLAMING RED HAIR

In his later years John Kelley, who had been captain of a wagon train, enjoyed relating an incident that occurred the first week out on the Oregon Trail.

"There was a woman driving a team and wagon and for company she had brought along her niece," he told. "We were only a hundred miles from Missouri when the woman died. No reason for it, just up and died. The niece was left completely alone.

"The girl was young, horribly scatter-brained and rather homely, too. None of the single men would have anything to do with her. Her only attribute seemed to be the beautiful head of bright red hair that she possessed. It hung in tight curls over her shoulders and down to the middle of her back.

"We crossed into Indian country with the girl driving her aunt's team. One day an Indian hunting party appeared. They showed no signs of hostility and I allowed them to ride alongside and keep us company. An Indian, mounted on a magnificent black horse, dropped back and rode beside the red-haired girl. He stared at her but never uttered a word.

"Did he see her as a beautiful goddess? I do not know. But the men, the same ones who had shunned her, now made objections. They told the lovesick brave they did not want him courting one of their women and expelled him from the wagon train. The girl watched her admirer ride over the ridge and commented to one of the women that all she wanted was a man who would worship her.

"That evening the Indian reappeared at the edge of camp. He and his horse stood still as a granite statue. A long moment passed and then the girl went running to him. The Indian reached for her and swung her up behind him. The coal black horse whirled and galloped away.

"At the top of the rise the girl turned back toward the circle of wagons. She waved. And that was the last anyone saw of the girl with the flaming red hair."

WHITE FEATHER

In his reminiscences James Neall related an experience he had on the Oregon Trail in 1848. His party was coming through buffalo country along the Platte River when James wrote that he saw "... a large Buffalo bull coming down on the opposite side of the river making for a low range of hills some half mile distant and on our side of the river. As I had never killed a buffalo entirely by myself, I was seized with the idea of killing him in order to say I had killed a buffalo.

"I took an English smooth bore flintlock musket instead of my rifle of small bore on account of it carrying a larger ball to execute my fell purpose. Having taken note of the direction the bull was taking I laid my course so as to intercept him. I proceeded about three-quarters of a mile and as I raised up on the top of one of the ridges, there was Mr. Bull about twenty yards off, standing broadside to me. I raised my musket, pulled the trigger, and down came the hammer but as the wind was blowing fresh right in my teeth the spark failed to ignite the power.

"The sound apparently made Mr. Bull aware of my presence. The shaggy monster stopped and glared at me. Instantly a thousand recollections of tales of a wounded bull in pursuit of a bad marksman flashed through me, and glancing behind me over a stretch of three-quarters of a mile between myself and camp I began to doubt my speed. Looking Mr. Bull in the face I apologized and said, 'It's all been a mistake. I intended no insult. You go your way and I'll go mine,' and he did. I confess to showing the 'white feather'."

THE FINAL INSULT

In the spring of 1850 a group of pioneers abandoned their homes in Wisconsin, formed a wagon train and started for Oregon. They did not encounter any Indians until they reached the Snake River.

John James, a small boy at the time, later wrote: "We set a very cozy camp and some of us youngsters went for a refreshing swim in the Snake River. There was plenty of fine grass for the stock. We never gave a thought to any danger that might exist and did not even post a guard that night. In the morning we awakened to find the stock scattered, a number missing, and could only guess they had been run off by Indians.

"A search party was organized and started in pursuit of the missing animals. Downriver, near the crossing, they came across the body of one of our largest oxen, Old Dave. He had been a very independent kind of an ox and I suppose he objected to being captured, tried to turn back and they had cut his throat.

"We only lost the one ox, but Mr. Robert Foster, traveling with one wagon, lost his entire team. There stood the wagon, wife and children, helpless in the wilds, a lonely-looking prospect staring them in the face. Our people contributed each what they could spare and re-outfitted Mr. Foster with a makeshift team.

"The thing that really got our goats was the way the Indians acted. They stayed in plain sight, on the opposite side of the river, just beyond rifle range, and tried all sorts of antics to provoke us to shoot. We could not even accept the challenge when they taunted us by stooping over and offering their backsides for targets."

FIRE SPIRIT

A group of Oregon Trail pioneers employed an Indian named Red Thunder to guide them across the Plains. At one point in the journey Red Thunder lay down and placed his ear against the ground.

Before swinging onto the back of his pony Red Thunder somberly stated, "Fire Spirit live in cloud. Afraid Fire Spirit him come awake."

At midday, while the pioneers were eating, the Indian walked a short distance from camp and again put his ear to the ground. He quickly leaped to his feet and searched the horizon until he spotted a tiny smudge of smoke far to the south.

Red Thunder jumped on his horse and announced, "Fire Spirit awake!" He led the others to the safety of a distant, rocky bald knob where grass did not grow. Soon the wind carried the acrid smell of smoke. Live embers were in the air. Spot fires began to ignite. Wild animals were fleeing. The heavens were black and suffocating smoke blocked the sun. Fire surged around the bald knob and swept past.

When the glorious sunshine returned to the blue sky, and fleecy white clouds once again rolled overhead it made the blackened landscape of the prairie all the more bleak and desolate.

MISSOURI MULE

William Jenkins was a boy of ten when his family headed west over the Oregon Trail. In his later years William would sometimes tell the story about the night he stood guard.

"Well, there we were," he would say, drawing out the words, "camped in the middle of nowhere. I had been pestering the men for weeks to allow me to stand guard. That particular night I suppose they figured we were out of Indian country because they gave in, although they left me with explicit instructions — saying that if anything of a suspicious nature, anything at all, happened during the night I was to signal by firing a shot in the air. One of them gave me an old blunderbuss and then they all turned in for the night.

"A sliver of moon came up and cast an eerie light. It was not enough to see anything by, only dim shadows. There were night sounds. A coyote howled and one of the dogs from the wagon train barked. A horse nickered and pawed the ground.

"Like I said, I couldn't see much of anything but I could clearly see this one Missouri mule in close to the fire. All at once that mule's ears shot forward, pointing into the dark like something was out there. Mules never lie. I cranked off a round and the camp was instantly in turmoil. Men dressed in longjohns, armed to the teeth, were up and running, looking for someone to shoot.

"I explained why I blazed away. They scolded me and said, 'The darn kid woke us up for nothing.' But the next morning they found an Indian hair rope down among the horses. Some Indian had evidently been fixing to steal the horses. I told them, I says, 'See, that old Missouri mule wasn't so dumb after all.'"

BAD FEELINGS

In the spring of 1847 one of the largest wagon trains to come west departed from the Missouri River. It consisted of more than one thousand wagons and five thousand pioneers. They were separated into thirty divisions. When all the wagons were underway, with spacing between the divisions, the wagon train stretched a distance of more than one hundred miles.

Included among the travelers were farmers, merchants, clergymen, doctors, college professors, lawyers and one future governor. Along the way lovers' vows were exchanged, vows were broken, babies were born and people died.

The divisions at the rear of the long wagon train endured the most trying conditions because those who preceded them had not maintained sanitary camping areas. And the loose stock — ten thousand head of cattle, one thousand horses and several hundred mules and sheep — had cut a swath twenty miles wide on either side of the trail, leaving little grass for those who followed.

But the most troubling of all were the Indians. They resented the large number of whites moving through their country and sought revenge against late arrivals.

Upon reaching The Dalles, the last divisions had to wait to arrange passage downriver or to begin the climb over the Cascades on Barlow's Trail. It was here the bad feelings between the whites and the Indians erupted into bloodshed. An emigrant became belligerent and was killed by an Indian. In retaliation several Indians, including a chief, were murdered.

HIDDEN STRENGTH

After the Oregon Trail pioneers had crossed nearly 2,000 miles the last leg of the journey often proved the most difficult. Standing in the way were the Cascades, an imposing range of snow-capped peaks. Travelers could either float their wagons down the Columbia River on rafts or traverse over the high pass on the flank of 11,239-foot Mt. Hood.

One group of Missouri pioneers elected to float the river and the wagons and passengers were crowded onto rafts. Six men were relegated to drive the stock overland along a difficult trail that paralleled the river.

The six men driving the animals stopped at a landing above a particularly dangerous section of the river to watch. At this point the river boiled with rapids and plunged over a series of short falls. There was only a narrow slot through which the rafts could pass safely.

One of the ferries was manned by an inexperienced crew and as they came toward the landing the current caught them and spun the raft headlong toward the dull roar and the rising mist of the cataracts. The passengers and crew cried out for help and one of them had presence of mind to throw a rope toward shore. But it uncoiled and fell short. The six men ran forward, waded into the water and formed a human chain with the last man able to grab the end of the rope.

The men on shore began a tug of war with the raft and, using every ounce of strength the six possessed, they were able to gain control of the raft. It began a gentle arc that brought it to shore only a few scant feet short of going over the waterfall.

PURE JOY

C.D. Barkhart and his family had crossed the Rocky Mountains in their covered wagon but were having difficulties as they labored over the high plains. They were thirsty and hungry. They were on rations of three swigs of water a day and had been without meat or flour for more than a week.

The situation was as desperate as it could be and adding to the family's misery was the oppressive heat that shimmered in waves and the choking dust that rose from the sandy soil. All of a sudden the oxen picked up their heads and began lumbering forward at a trot. They had smelled the Snake River and they did not stop running until they were standing in the cool water.

The animals and the Barkharts satisfied their thirst. Camp was struck there on the riverbank and the sun began to set. Clouds along the western horizon turned gold and crimson.

Facing another long night with hunger gnawing at their bellies brought the Barkharts together. They got down on their knees and thanked God for the water that had slaked their thirst and then they prayed for something to eat.

One of the children cried out, "Antelope! I see an antelope!" The child pointed and there, skylined on the ridge, was an antelope. C.D. grabbed his rifle, took careful aim and the concussion and booming crash of the rifle washed over the family. Up on the ridge top the antelope fell dead.

PLAYING INDIAN

The Griffin family started west by wagon in the spring of 1880. They traveled in the company of four other families who had children about the same ages as the seven Griffin children.

A favorite game the children loved to play in camp was called Indian. It was a simple game; some of the children were pioneers and the others were Indians. The ones who were playing Indians would hide in the sagebrush and come running off a side hill throwing sticks as if they were make-believe spears and arrows.

The small wagon train reached Southern Oregon. The long journey was nearly over. One morning, while the adults were busy breaking camp after breakfast, the children busied themselves playing a game of Indian.

On this morning little Annie Griffin was an Indian. She came running off the side hill, whooping as savagely as she could. One of her sisters, a pioneer, ran from Annie, trying to escape by crawling up into the wagon box. Annie went after her.

An older brother had carelessly placed his pistols on the bed in the wagon and as Annie appeared in the opening at the back of the wagon her sister grabbed the pistol, pointed it at Annie, and pulled the trigger. There was a flash of fire and a tremendous boom as the weapon discharged.

Luckily the slug missed Annie. It continued on, whizzing within a few scant inches of Mrs. Griffin who was holding her baby in her arms, finally becoming embedded in the wooden rail of a nearby wagon.

Never again were the children allowed to play Indian.

SHEEPMAN

At the age of 26 David Stump, a surveyor and teacher, gave up on life in Iowa and sought a new beginning in Oregon. David had no wagon and no money, but he was able to convince the captain of a wagon train to take him along after giving an exhibition of his skill as a marksman. David walked all the way to Oregon and paid his way by shooting wild game to supply fresh meat for the pioneers.

The wagon train arrived in the Willamette Valley in the fall of 1846. Two years later gold was discovered at Sutter's Mill and David was lured to the California gold fields. He spent a year at the diggings and in that time managed to accumulate a sizable fortune. Then he journeyed east and purchased a large flock of sheep that he, with several herders, started over the Oregon Trail.

At the Snake River David arranged for a group of Indians to use their canoes to help guide the sheep to the opposite side. For their help David promised them all the sheep that drowned in the process. The crossing went smoothly until it seemed that a great number of sheep were drowning. David watched closely and discovered the Indians were paddling alongside the swimming sheep and slyly holding their heads under water.

But the majority of the flock did make it to shore and David and the herders started west again. They reached the Willamette Valley and David had enough gold remaining in his saddlebags to purchase 2,300 acres of choice grasslands. Thereafter David Stump was known as the "Father of the Sheep Industry in Oregon".

BUFFALO STAMPEDE

Even though George Himes was only nine years old, his parents allowed him to ride his horse ahead of the wagon train. One day as they were crossing the Plains, George was a good mile ahead of the first wagon. After topping a slight rise, he looked out and saw a thin layer of what looked to be fog along the western horizon. It took the boy a moment to realize what it actually was, and he immediately turned back and raced toward the wagons at a gallop. When he was within earshot he hollered, "Buffalo! Buffalo stampede!"

"Circle the wagons!" commanded the captain. There was no time to waste and the lead wagon came around to meet the last. The men worked to unhitch the oxen and bring them, as well as the loose stock, inside the wagon corral.

The rumble of thousands of hooves striking the ground became audible and soon the advancing herd could be seen, surging across the Plains like a huge, brown river. The herd passed to one side of the circle of wagons, so dangerously close that occasionally the choking dust would part to reveal an individual cow or bull, foaming at the mouth, breath coming short and fast.

George Himes related that it took more than an hour for the herd to pass and that as the dust slowly began to settle it was discovered the buffalo had continued on for a quarter-mile. The stampede had ended at a cliff above the Platte River where thousands of buffalo had plunged over the edge to their death.

FRIENDS

This is a story about two boys, one named Sitton and the other Fendall, and how they happened to meet and become lifelong friends.

Sitton signed on with a wagon train coming west. He was a likeable kid and got along with everyone. But all that changed the night he stood guard. On that night he might have been a little jumpy, or maybe his eyesight was not real good because he thought he saw an Indian attempting to steal the horses. He fired one quick shot.

"I got him!" Sitton hollered.

This caused quite a commotion in the camp. A company of men, armed with rifles and carrying lanterns, went to have a look and discovered the kid had killed the wagon train captain's favorite mule.

The angry captain told Sitton, "Pack up what you can carry and head east. You're hereby banished from this wagon train."

Several days behind the wagon train was a second wagon train. Charley Fendall, a member of this group, was riding in front when he spotted a young man afoot, traveling east. The paths of the two had finally crossed and Sitton climbed up behind Fendall and they rode double on his horse. From that moment the two were inseparable friends. They eventually made it to Oregon and spent the first winter in a cabin on Panther Creek. In spring they staked out adjoining land claims, married sisters and remained friends for the rest of their days.

THE ARROW

An hour of daylight remained when the wagon train captain turned in his saddle and made a circular motion with his free hand. This was the signal for the drivers to circle the wagons.

The pioneers were wary because they knew they were approaching Indian country. Their worst fears were confirmed when one of the men discovered a message scratched into the sun-bleached skull of a buffalo. It stated, "Indians hostile".

After the animals had been cared for and the pioneers had eaten supper the captain called a meeting. His instructions were to the point. He stated, "We have to assume any Indian we see is hostile. I want all the fires extinguished so as not to attract attention to ourselves and we will double the usual number of guards."

At one of the campfires a girl was hurrying to mend her brother's trousers. She screamed suddenly and fell over. An arrow was embedded in her thigh.

The fire was immediately extinguished and the girl was taken to a wagon. Heavy blankets were thrown over the bows to shield it while emergency surgery was performed by lantern light. The arrow was removed and it was discovered that the girl's leg bone had been broken. The leg was set in a temporary splint with two ramrods.

In the morning the wound was treated, the leg set properly and the wagon train went on its way, trying to hurry through the hostile Indian country.

THANK THE OX

Perhaps it was the quick alarm of a rattlesnake or maybe only the wind making a strange sound through the sage, but something startled a pair of grazing oxen and sent them stampeding into the Snake River. The current was deceptive and it quickly carried them downstream.

Pioneer John Southerlin, a large athletic man, never hesitated. He kicked off his boots and dove into the swirling water. He circled around the oxen and by yelling and splashing water with his hands he succeeded in turning the oxen back to shore.

By then John was beginning to flounder. He did not have enough remaining strength to pull himself free of the clutches of the Snake.

A voice boomed out across the water. It was Porter Wilson, one of the other emigrants who saw what was happening and had chased along the bank to keep up with the action. He hollered, "Grab that ox by the tail."

With a great amount of exertion John was able to swim to the nearest ox and grab hold of its tail. The ox pulled him to shore.

Later, John graciously thanked Porter for saving his life. But Porter told him, "Don't thank me. I never got wet. Thank the ox."

JUSTICE SERVED

In 1845 Caleb Greenwood and his three sons met a group of emigrants at Fort Hall on the Snake River and tried to persuade them to abandon their Oregon dream and take the cutoff to California.

Eight wagons broke away from the wagon train and followed the Greenwoods. After three days of traveling Caleb left his oldest son John in charge of guiding the wagons while he returned to Fort Hall to persuade more emigrants to follow.

The following day an Indian jumped up from behind a clump of sagebrush and scared John's horse. The horse reared and nearly threw John to the ground. This infuriated the young man. He snarled, "I'll kill him," as he pulled his rifle from the scabbard.

"He didn't mean no harm. Don't shoot 'im," one of the pioneers called. And when it looked as though John intended to defy him and shoot anyway he called to the Indian, "Run for your life!" But the Indian only made it a few steps before being shot in the back.

That night Caleb Greenwood rode into camp. He was angry. "I came across an Indian who had been shot in the back. The man who shot him is a murderer and he should hang."

John, who had positioned himself at the outer perimeter of camp, jumped on his horse and escaped. But in the long run justice was served. Not long after this incident John was involved in a fight over a game of cards and was stabbed to death.

REMEMBERING

Benjamin Bonney was a seven-year-old boy when he came over the Oregon Trail in 1845. His most vivid memories of the ordeal were when they departed Independence, Missouri, the last settlement, and the nights they were trapped on the plains during frightening thunderstorms.

"We passed through Independence, the last trading point on the frontier, and there were a number of wagon shops and blacksmith shops, as well as livery stables and hotels. The Indians were camped all around the settlement and were anxious to trade buffalo robes for shirts, powder, lead, or firewater.

"But what I remember most vividly, the thing that scared me most were the thunderstorms. When they rolled in during the night the oxen had to be chained together so they could not stampede. Sometimes the wind blew so hard our tents would be flattened and the covers torn off the wagons. Then the rain would come down and we would be like drowning rats.

"Unless you have been through a storm on the Great Plains, you have no idea how scary and confusing it can be. The oxen bellowing, children crying, women whispering to not be afraid, men shouting and the thunder rolling like a constant salvo of artillery. One second it was bright as day, and the next black as the depths of a pit."

SLEEPLESS NIGHT

The Pringle family came across the Oregon Trail in 1846, but veered away from the main route to take the Applegate Cutoff across the desert and through Southern Oregon to the Willamette Valley.

It was late in the fall before the Pringle family reached the Umpqua Valley. Only one horse was still alive and, facing starvation, it was decided 14-year-old Octavius must ride to the Willamette Valley and bring back supplies.

Octavius made the journey, purchased dried peas and wheat graham flour, all he thought the poor mare could carry, and led her back toward his starving family. As he was coming along the mountainous trail Octavius came upon a bear track. It was fresh; muddy water was still filtering into it. For five miles he tagged along behind the bear and then, just before dark, it wandered off the trail. That night Octavius curled up in his blanket and slept fitfully, dreaming about the bear.

He awakened with a start to sounds crashing in the nearby brush and faster than greased lightning Octavius shinnied up a fir tree. He perched there on a limb for the remainder of the night. Each time he thought about coming down he would hear branches crack and he knew the bear was still there, waiting for him.

At first light he discovered the cause of his fright was not the bear at all but an old emaciated emigrant cow left behind to die. He drove the bag of bones away and with utmost disgust he hit the trail. Two days later he found his family and a feast of boiled peas and graham bread was prepared. The Pringles reached the Willamette Valley and settled on land near Eugene Skinner, the founder of Eugene.

TOUGH

Elizabeth Geer brought her husband and their seven children across the plains to Oregon. When they reached the settlement of Portland Elizabeth sold the wagon and stock to pay rent on a lean-to shed off the back of a cabin. Her husband, who was sick and confined to bed, had to be carried to their new quarters.

Every night Elizabeth prayed that her husband would get well and that life would become easier. But the prayers were not answered. Food was expensive and scarce: pork cost ten cents a pound and potatoes were seventy-five cents per bushel. But the Indians sold salmon for four cents a pound and the family subsisted on a diet of fish.

Adding to Elizabeth's concerns were the children. They became sick. At one time five of them were down, too sick to move, and all Elizabeth could do was to make them comfortable and hope for the best. She could not afford to pay for a doctor's care.

On the first day of February 1849 Elizabeth wrote in her diary: "This day my dear husband, my last remaining friend, died."

The following day she entered, "Today we buried my earthly companion. Now I know what none but widows know; that is, how comfortless is a widow's life; especially when left in a strange land without money or friends, and the care of seven children."

THAT WINTER

The Ross family immigrated to Oregon in 1862. They claimed a homestead along the lower Columbia River but when spring came their farm flooded and they were forced to move to higher ground.

Charles Ross, who had been a small boy at the time, recalled, "We were isolated, seven miles to the closest neighbors and no wagon road, no trail, it was all by rowboat.

"The first winter we spent there it got terrible cold early on and Father went out and brought back a supply of flour. The river froze behind him. Then on top of the cold it started to snow. It would thaw a little during the day, snow in the evening and freeze again at night. Snow built up to four feet deep.

"The worst part was we started the winter with fifty head of cattle and only three ton of wild marsh hay. Father had figured the steers would be able to range for themselves while the hay was intended for the cows that would be calving. The hay was soon gone and Father resorted to chopping down maple trees so the cattle could eat the twigs. When a tree would fall, how the cattle would flounder through the snow for it.

"But even with this minimal feed the cattle soon began to die. The cold snap lasted three months. We lost half the cattle.

"After such a winter the folks were disheartened at what we had been forced to endure and were determined not to pass another such winter. We packed up, moved to the settlement of Portland and Dad got a regular job."

THE BOY AND THE SHADOW

After the Civil War the Krewson family decided to leave the troubled times behind and move west to Oregon. Several neighboring families joined in and they formed a small wagon company.

As the wagon train was crossing the Great Plains they came across a grisly scene. Indians had attacked the wagon train ahead of them and all the men, women and children had been massacred. It was so fresh the wagon remains were still smoldering. All they could do was bury the dead and continue on.

When the company reached the Blue Mountains the men went on a hunting expedition and they were able to kill a number of deer. A feast was held that night.

One of the Krewson boys, who was barely fourteen years old, had been begging to take a turn as night guard. Since they had not seen any Indians for a number of days the boy was told he would get his wish, that he would take the first guard shift. While the others slept the boy paced back and forth, feeling very grown up and self-important.

Something, a shadow in the moonlight, moved. The boy watched the shadow creep forward, stop and creep forward again.

"Halt!" the boy shouted. The shadow moved and the boy fired his rifle. Fire licked at the night.

The camp was thrown into an uproar. Men crowded around the Krewson boy and demanded to know what he was shooting at. The boy led them to the dark shadow at the edge of camp. There they found not an Indian, but a dead black bear. Apparently it had been attracted by the smell of the venison feast.

THE OLD MAN OF THE TRAIL

Ezra Meeker first came to the Oregon Country in 1852, crossing the Oregon Trail by wagon and oxen team. Fifty-four years later he proposed to retrace the route and mark it with a series of trail markers to preserve it for future generations.

Meeker solicited money in Portland for his trip, but received only $200. The general feeling in that city was no one wanted to contribute to a fund sending a 76-year-old man on a trip which most likely would kill him. But Meeker was determined. He hitched a pair of oxen named Twist and Dave to a wagon and started east.

The small towns across Eastern Oregon gave Meeker rousing welcomes. The school children went on penny drives, collecting pennies to give to Meeker. At Boise a crowd of 3,000 turned out for a parade led by Twist and Dave.

From the end of the trail to the Great Plains, Meeker raised more than one hundred cedar trail markers. His plans were to continue his trek all the way to Washington, D.C., where he would ask the President for help in establishing more markers. But in Nebraska the faithful ox Twist died and the journey was interrupted while Meeker hiked to the Omaha stockyards to purchase a five-year-old steer he named Dandy.

On November 29, 1907, with Dave and Dandy dodging the traffic on Pennsylvania Avenue, Meeker realized his dream by driving his wagon onto the front lawn of the White House. President Teddy Roosevelt came out to pose with the outfit and the colorful white-bearded pioneer.

Meeker made one more trip over the Oregon Trail before his death in 1928 at the age of 98. He flew the route in an airplane.

Rick Steber's Tales of the Wild West Series is available in hardbound and paperback books featuring illustrations by Don Gray, as well as audio narrated by Dallas McKennon. Current titles in the series include:

OREGON TRAIL Vol. 1 *
PACIFIC COAST Vol. 2 *
INDIANS Vol. 3 *
COWBOYS Vol. 4 *
WOMEN OF THE WEST Vol. 5 *
CHILDREN'S STORIES Vol. 6 *
LOGGERS Vol. 7 *
MOUNTAIN MEN Vol. 8 *
MINERS Vol. 9 *
GRANDPA'S STORIES Vol. 10
PIONEERS Vol. 11
CAMPFIRE STORIES Vol. 12
TALL TALES Vol. 13
GUNFIGHTERS Vol. 14
GRANDMA'S STORIES Vol. 15
Available on Audio Tape

Other books written by Rick Steber—

NO END IN SIGHT	*HEARTWOOD*
BUY THE CHIEF A CADILLAC	*ROUNDUP*
BUCKAROO HEART	*LAST OF THE PIONEERS*
NEW YORK TO NOME	*TRACES*
WILD HORSE RIDER	*RENDEZVOUS*

If unavailable at local retailers, write directly to the publisher for a free catalog.

Bonanza Publishing
Box 204
Prineville, Oregon 97754